Mind Your
MANNERS

For my mum, who made
sure I was a polite panda
(even if I'm still a messy monkey!)
~ NE

For all of my grandparents
~ FPT

CATERPILLAR BOOKS
An imprint of the Little Tiger Group
www.littletiger.co.uk
1 Coda Studios, 189 Munster Road, London SW6 6AW
First published in Great Britain 2018 • This edition published 2019
Text by Nicola Edwards • Text copyright © Caterpillar Books Ltd. 2018
Illustrations copyright © Feronia Parker Thomas 2018
A CIP catalogue record for this book is available from the British Library
All rights reserved • Printed in China
ISBN: 978-1-84857-889-0
CPB/1400/1114/0419
1 3 5 7 9 10 8 6 4 2

Mind Your
MANNERS

Written by
Nicola Edwards

Illustrated by
Feronia Parker Thomas

Just look at this place! It's a nightmare!
All this squawking and squealing and tears...
Now everyone, just stop right there!
And all of you, prick up your ears.

If we want to be happy together,
We need to have all of the tools.
Good manners make life so much better.
They're not just some silly old rules.

Now no one likes **mean**, greedy grabbers.
I'm sure everybody agrees.

You won't get far being a **snatcher**,
Polite pandas always say "please"!

Rude tigers soon stop getting presents.
So when somebody does something nice,
Just say "thank you", smile and be pleasant.
You might find good things happen twice.

There's no need to stomp, clomp and crash by.
You don't have to barge past so rudely.

One small, simple trick that you must try,
Is to tap people and say "excuse me".

We all make a mess of things sometimes,
But if you've been a silly old snake,

Don't dither and slither,
have a strong spine!

And say "sorry"
when you make a mistake.

We share this world with one another,
So let's make it a **friendlier** place.

There's no need to go **squashing** each other,
Just like you, we all need our own space.

We don't have to start squawking like parrots.
Learn the meaning of words, don't be crude.

SQUAWK

SQUAWK

So you don't end up getting in trouble,
For parroting words that are rude!

Dropping rubbish and upsetting nature

Is not clever, cool, funny or big.

We all need to be good team players.
What's the use of one more selfish pig?

Even if you're the messiest monkey,
Close your mouth when you're munching your food.
No one wants to catch sight of your tonsils,
Or your lunch when it's mashed up and chewed.

If you want to be one of the cool cats,
Do try not to gross people out.
Don't shower your friends with a snot splat,
Or go sneezing your germs all about.

It's unkind to hurt anyone's feelings,
So take care with the words that you speak.

Sing out all you like about sweet things.
But keep mean nasty stuff in your beak!

It's okay to enjoy roaring loudly.
We all deserve some time to play.

But all lions should **practise** those **soft growls**
For the **quieter times** of the day.

It's a **miserable life** being crabby,
Like a grouchy old grizzly bear.

Being unkind makes people unhappy,
So be good to each other, and share.

See how **good manners** make our lives nicer?

Why not brighten up everyone's day?

Just look at this place! It's **delightful**!

Full of **laughter** and **friendship** and **play**.